HOW DID YOUR CHINESE ANCESTORS LIVE?

Ancient China Life, Myth and Art Children's Ancient History

BABY PROFESSOR
EDUCATION KIDS

Speedy Publishing LLC
40 E. Main St. #1156
Newark, DE 19711
www.speedypublishing.com
Copyright 2017

All Rights reserved. No part of this book may be reproduced or used in any way or form or by any means whether electronic or mechanical, this means that you cannot record or photocopy any material ideas or tips that are provided in this book.

How did people live in long-ago China? What did they eat? What did they wear? Read on and learn more about how people lived in ancient China.

YELLOW RIVER

Six Thousand Years of Culture

Chinese culture began to develop over 6,000 years ago along the Yellow River valley. The society was based on honoring one's ancestors, the gods, and the local spirits, and also honoring other people. Chinese people believed there were spirits everywhere around them, and that they should live and act as if the spirits were watching.

The earliest Chinese societies seem to have been led by women who were also the religious leaders. The first central government in China was the Xia Dynasty, around 2000 BCE. They were followed by the Shang Dynasty (1600-1046 BCE). The earliest written records we have of how people lived are from the Shang Dynasty.

BEIJING OLD CITY TOWER

18TH CENTURY, SILK, GOLD THREAD, EMBROIDERY

SOCIAL CLASS

As in most of the rest of the world, how you lived in ancient China depended on whether you were high-class and wealthy, or low-class and poor. For example, silk became available as clothing long before the Shang Dynasty, but the people who processed the silkworm threads into cloth were not allowed to wear silk! Not even the people who sold the silk clothing could wear it. Only the rich who could afford to buy it could wear it. Everybody else wore clothing made of hemp.

Later, in the Sui Dynasty, an emperor passed a law that peasants (poor people who worked as farmers, or doing manual labor) could only wear blue or black clothing. Only rich people could wear colorful clothing!

You were born into your social class. If your father was a peasant, then that's what you were, too. Once writing was developed, it became even harder to rise from being a peasant, because only people of the upper classes could learn to read and write.

A CHINESE PUPIL

IMPERIAL EXAMINATION

THE IMPERIAL EXAMINATIONS

One way to rise in social class, if you could find a way to learn to read and write, was to pass the Imperial Examinations, which started in the Shang Dynasty. These tests were very hard, and to pass them you had to memorize a lot of information. Once you passed the tests, you could study for an interesting career, or take a job in the government.

FROM HEAD TO TOES

HAIR STYLES

Chinese men and women all wore their hair long. They felt it showed disrespect to your ancestors to have short hair. Upper-class women pinned their hair up with pins made of gold or ivory, while poor women could only make a knot of their hair, or tie it with string.

AN UPPER-CLASS CHINESE WOMAN

ANCIENT PERFUME SPRINKLERS

BODY ODOR

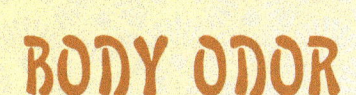

The Chinese thought that smelling sweaty and unwashed was what criminals and barbarians (people from other nations) smelled like. People used perfumes and deodorants on their bodies, and sucked cloves to improve the smell of their breath; but they thought it was dangerous to bathe too often, so people only had a bath every five days or so.

SHOES AND FEET

The rich wore shoes made of silk, while the poor wore boots and sandals made of straw, wood, and hemp. When people were at home, they wore slippers.

Around 900 CE, foot binding became a custom for the daughters of the wealthy. People felt that a really beautiful woman would have tiny feet.

CHINESE SHOES FOR BOUND FEET

A CHINESE WOMAN WITH DEFORMED FOOT

This practice, which involved distorting the feet with tight wrappings and even removing the smallest toes, spread through Chinese society. Even women who would work all their lives cultivating rice might have feet bound so tightly that they could barely walk.

SIGNS OF WEALTH

The rich wore fine jewellery, including rings and necklaces, and rich women also pinned the pretty wings of beetles to their clothing. Some men and women of the upper classes let their fingernails grow long as a sign that they were too important and powerful to do any work with their hands! Their servants would have to do everything for them, including feeding them and helping them get dressed.

A WEALTHY CHINESE MAN

CHINESE RICE FARMERS

FARMING AND FOOD

In China, rice was the main crop. People ate it at every meal, and could even pay their taxes with it.

Chinese people rarely ate meat, and followed a vegetarian diet with the addition of eggs and fish. People cooked in a pot called a ding, which stood over the fire on three legs.

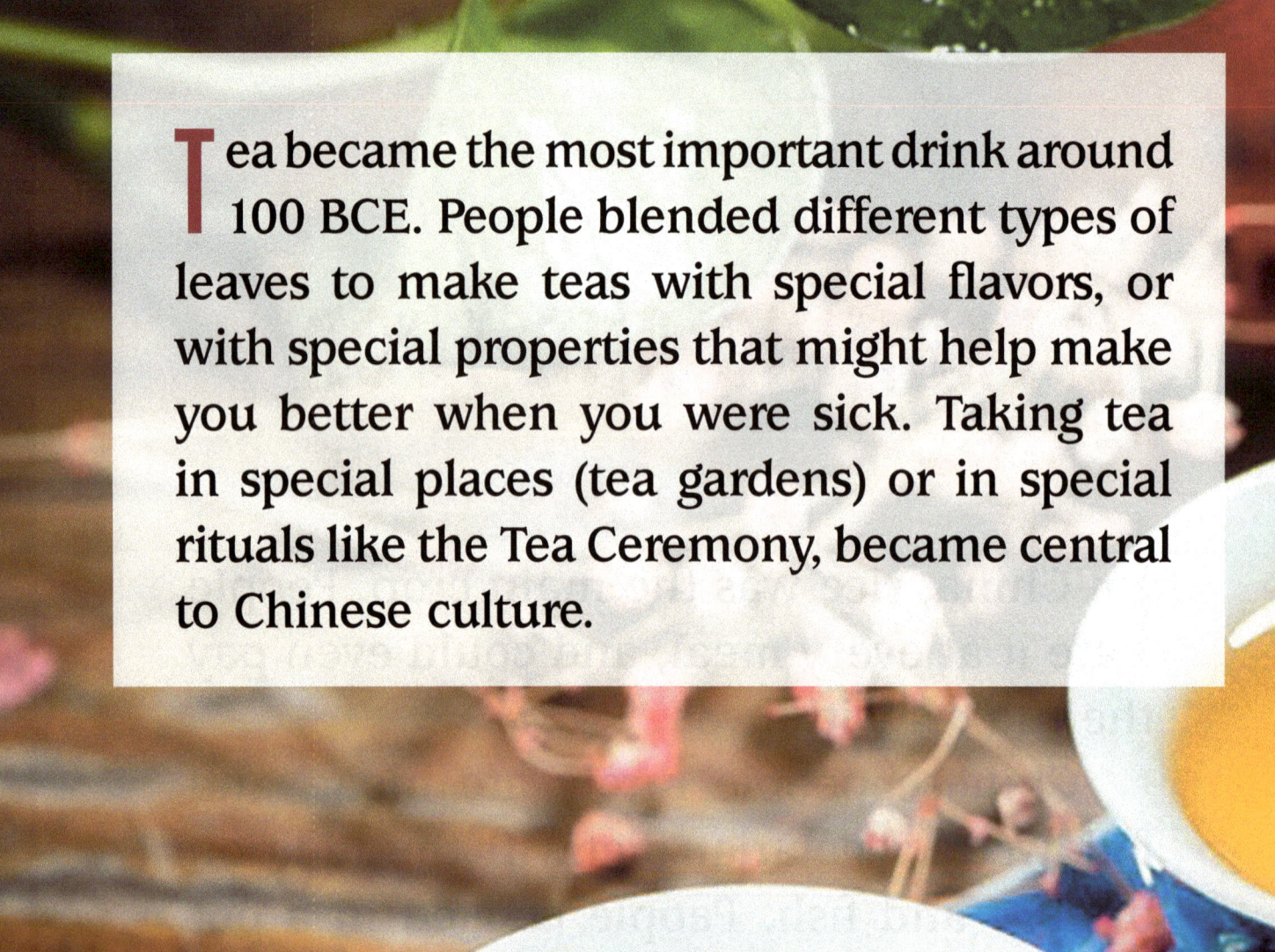

Tea became the most important drink around 100 BCE. People blended different types of leaves to make teas with special flavors, or with special properties that might help make you better when you were sick. Taking tea in special places (tea gardens) or in special rituals like the Tea Ceremony, became central to Chinese culture.

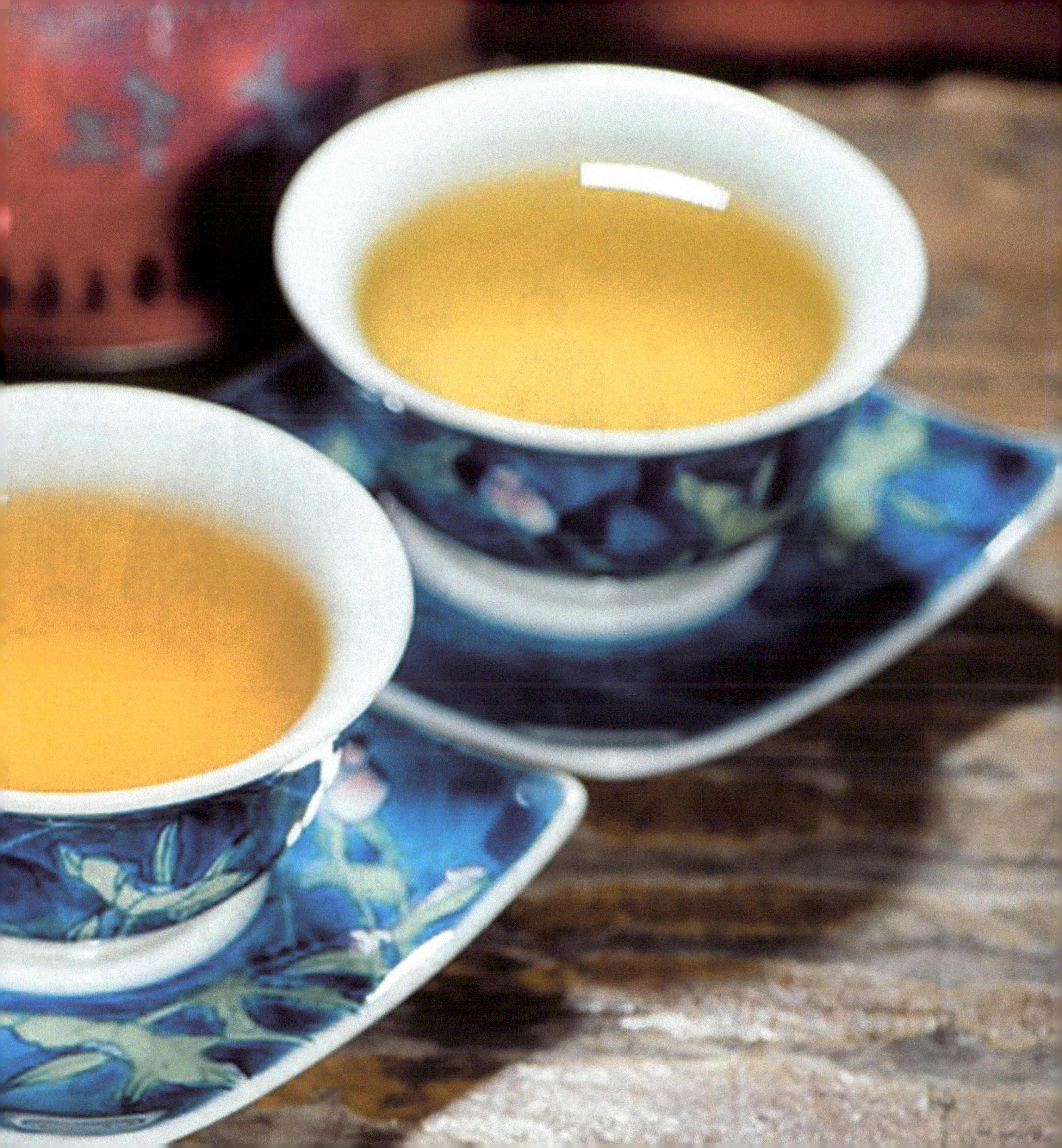

EVERYDAY LIFE IN OLD CHINA

LIFE AT HOME

The home was the center of family life, both for the rich and the poor. Women were in charge of the home while men worked outside the house.

In the peasant class, men, women, and children all worked together in the fields.

For the poor, the home might be a hut made of mud and sticks. Middle-class families had houses of wood built around an open courtyard. For the rich, how big and fancy their home was depended on how much money they wanted to spend on it.

PETS

In China, cats were the most popular pets. Almost every home had a cat. People kept dogs mainly for protection, and sometimes to eat.

RICH CHINESE FAMILY

A CHINESE GOD

RELIGION

Chinese religion honors the family's ancestors, the Tudi Gong (spirits of the earth), and great gods like Xi Wang Mu, The Mother of the West. Shangti was the supreme god, and was sometimes called The Yellow Emperor. He gave culture to the people. Cai Shen was the god of wealth. There were many festivals and rituals when people gathered at shrines or temples to honor the gods.

The idea of ghosts is common in Chinese culture, and overlaps with religious practice, as it was felt that the dead, who went to live with the gods, could influence the gods to help (or at least not hurt) the family. A family that did not honor its ancestors might be haunted by them.

A CHINESE GHOST PAINTING

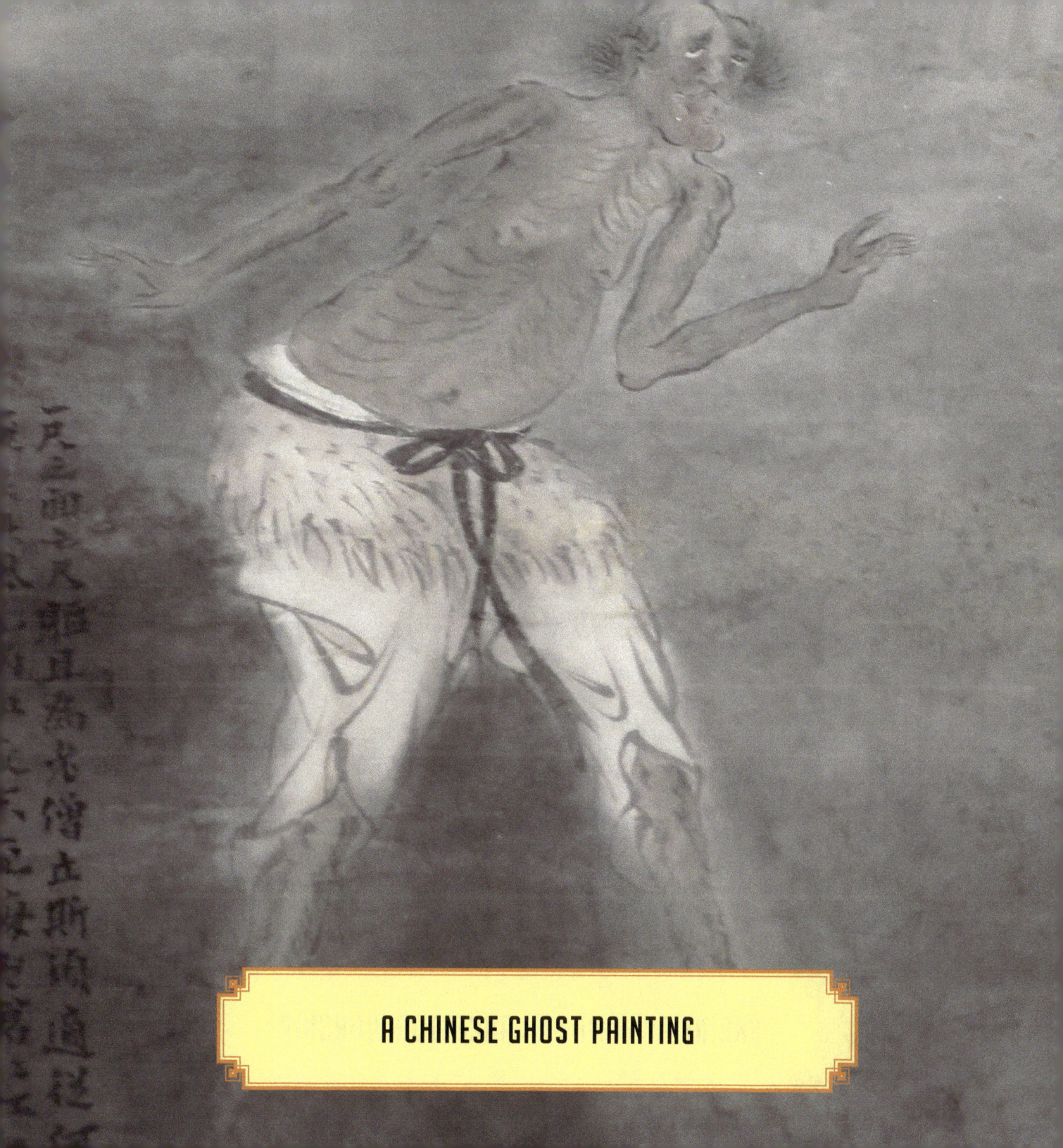

SHRINE AT HOME FOR ANCESTOR WORSHIP

A SHRINE OR TWO

Every home had a shrine, a place where the family honored their ancestors, the local gods of the land, and major gods that that family prayed to.

In the kitchen, there would also be a paper picture of Zao Shen, the "kitchen god". Zao Shen would report to the other gods how the family was doing at the end of each year, so the family would make sacrifices to Zao Shen so he would make a good report.

CHINESE KITCHEN GOD

BURNING THE KITCHEN GOD'S PICTURE IS A CHINESE TRADITION.

At the end of the year the family would burn the kitchen god's picture, and the oldest and most honored woman in the family would create a new picture to hang in the kitchen for the coming year.

EDUCATION

Only boys and men studied and became educated in ancient China. Girls were supposed to stay home and learn to be mothers and to run the house.

A CHINESE OLD BOOK

聖孔子
名丘字仲尼山東
兗州府曲阜縣人

CONFUCIUS

However, everyone was supposed to know the Five Virtues that Confucius taught, and these are the basis for Chinese education. The Five Virtues are:

- ★ Li, or manners
- ★ Ren, or kindness
- ★ Xin, or loyalty
- ★ Yi, or honesty
- ★ Zhi, moral knowledge so you understand what is right and what is wrong

Before paper was invented, around 100 BCE, students wrote on wooden sticks bound together into scrolls. In the Tang Dynasty (starting in 618 CE), people printed books using carved blocks of wood to press the ink onto paper, and this made it possible to print study materials for schools.

WOODEN BOOK

TRADITIONAL CHINESE MEDICINES

HEALTH AND MEDICINE

Since only men could learn to read and write in ancient China, almost all doctors were men. Women in rural areas could help sick people using herbs and traditional healing.

Before the Tang Dynasty, people believed that illness was caused by evil spirits. When Buddhism came to China, Buddhist priests ran "Fields of Compassion", which were like hospitals, old-age homes, and counselling centers.

BUDDHISM IN CHINA

EMPEROR TAIZONG

Emperor Taizong (626-649) established the first medical schools and demanded a high standard of conduct and results from doctors. In order to become a doctor, you had to pass the Imperial Examinations. Medical knowledge began to be taught and passed along in a systematic manner, by teachers at the medical schools and in books that doctors could refer to.

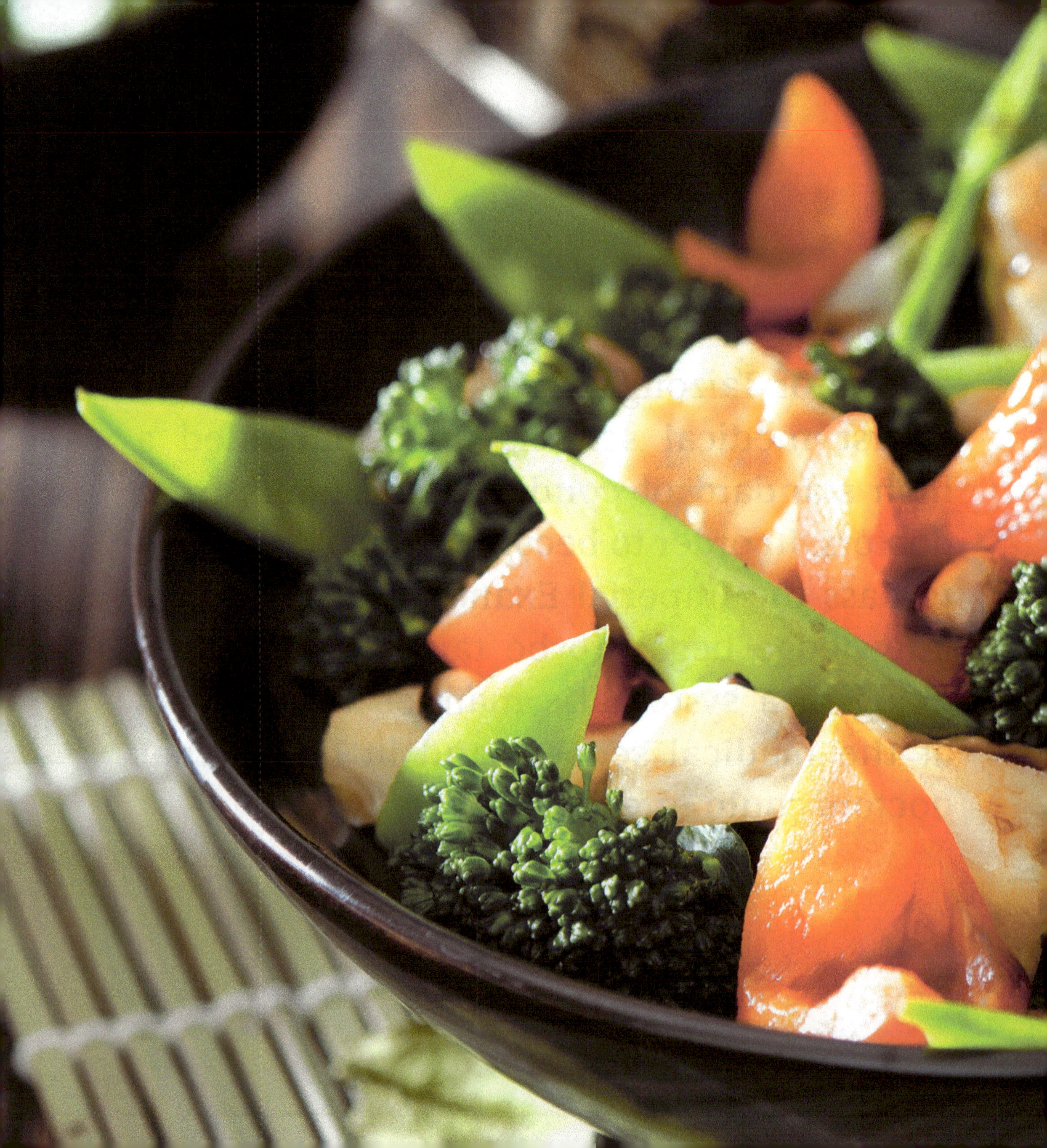

Chinese society has always valued a long, healthy, productive life. Chinese people were urged to follow a style of life, and a mainly-vegetarian diet, that would keep them healthy and keep their lives in balance.

FESTIVALS

Chinese culture developed many festivals and annual celebrations to mark the passage of the year. They also gave families a chance to celebrate and have a meal together instead of spending all day at work. Some of these festivals, like the Spring Festival and the Dragon Boat Festival, continue to be celebrated today.

RED LANTERNS DURING CHINESE NEW YEAR FESTIVAL

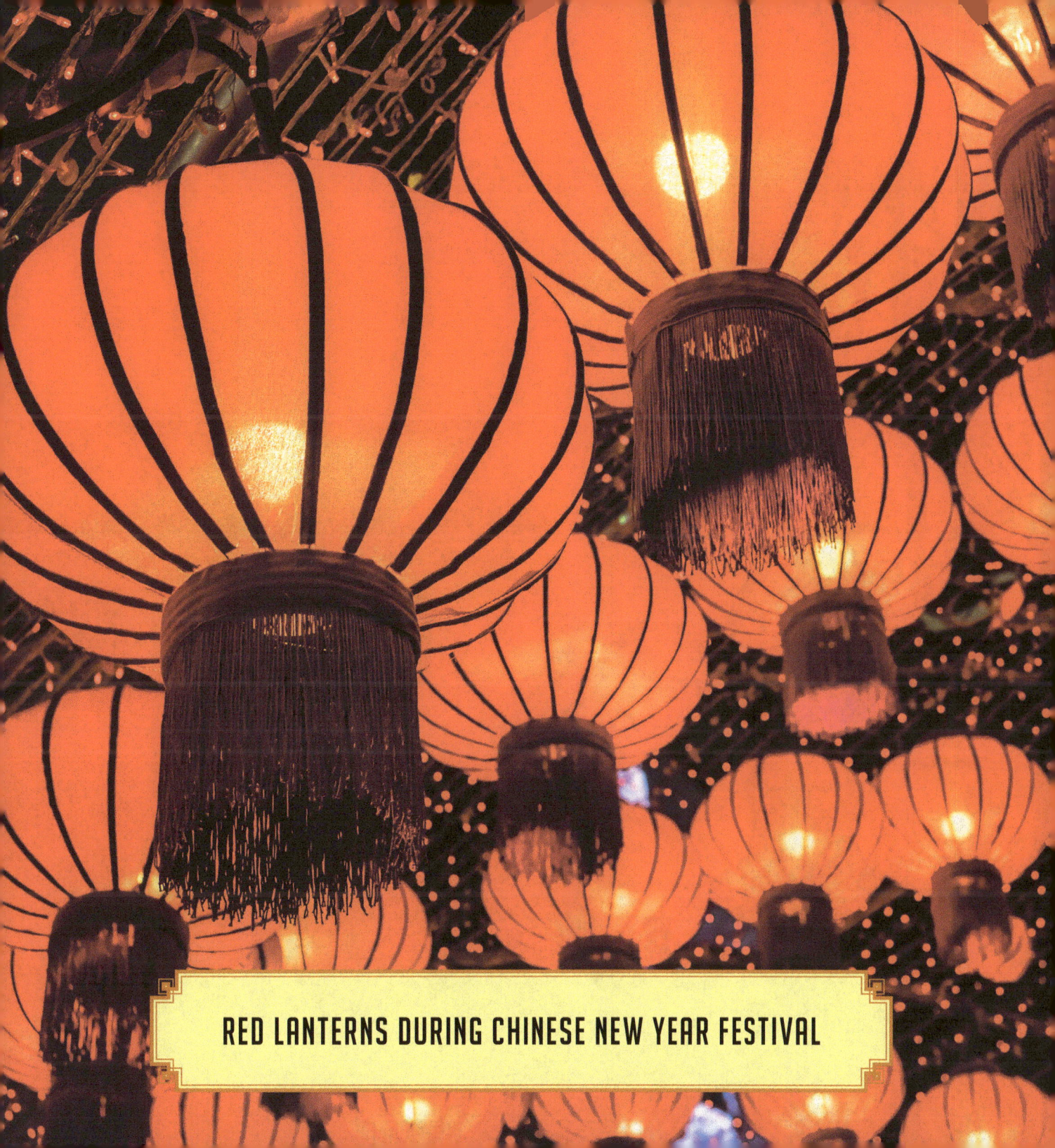

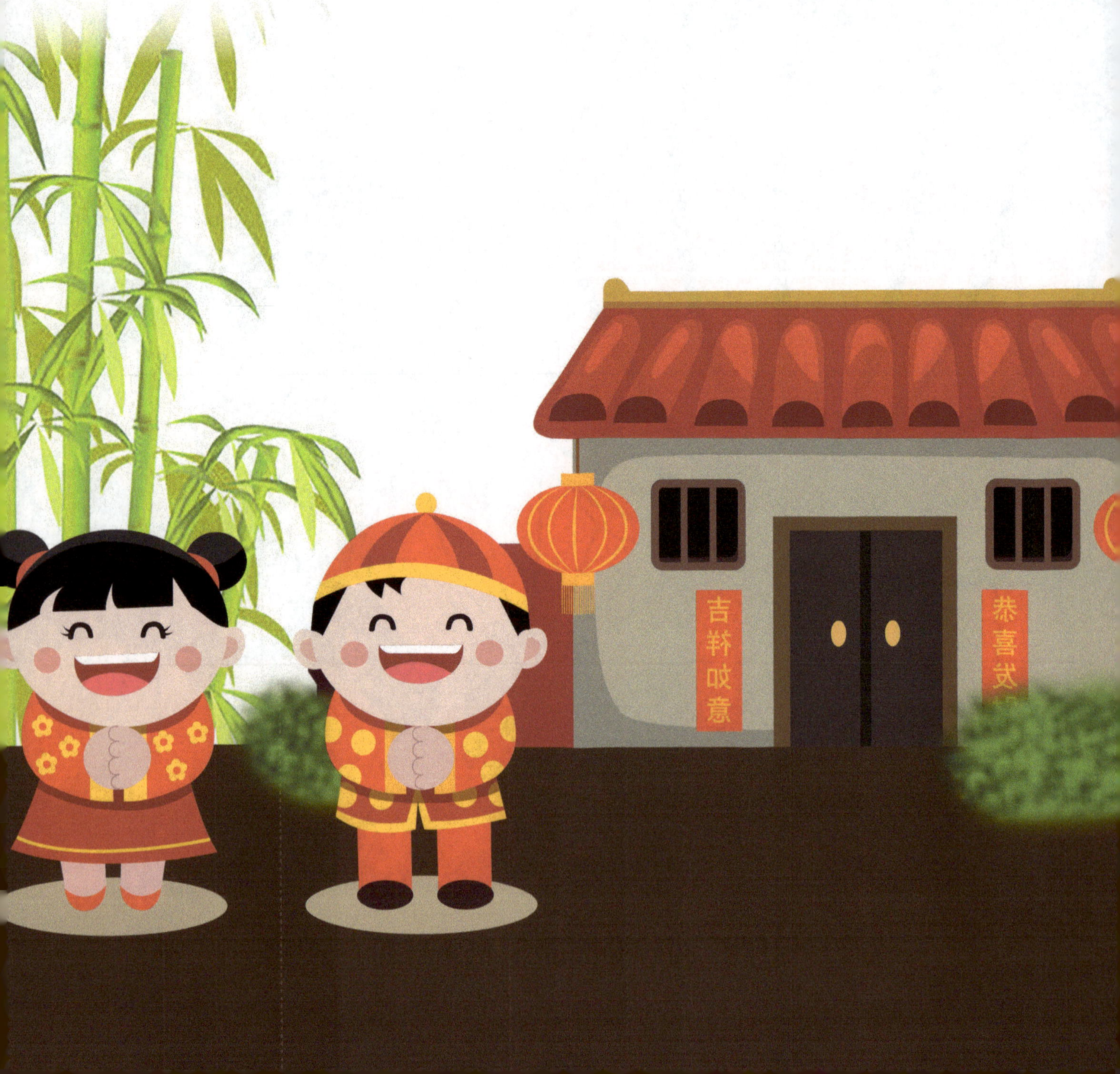
吉祥如意
恭喜发

There is much to learn about Chinese life and culture! Read other Baby Professor books, like Who Built the Great Wall of China? and Trade and Commerce in Ancient China, to find out more.

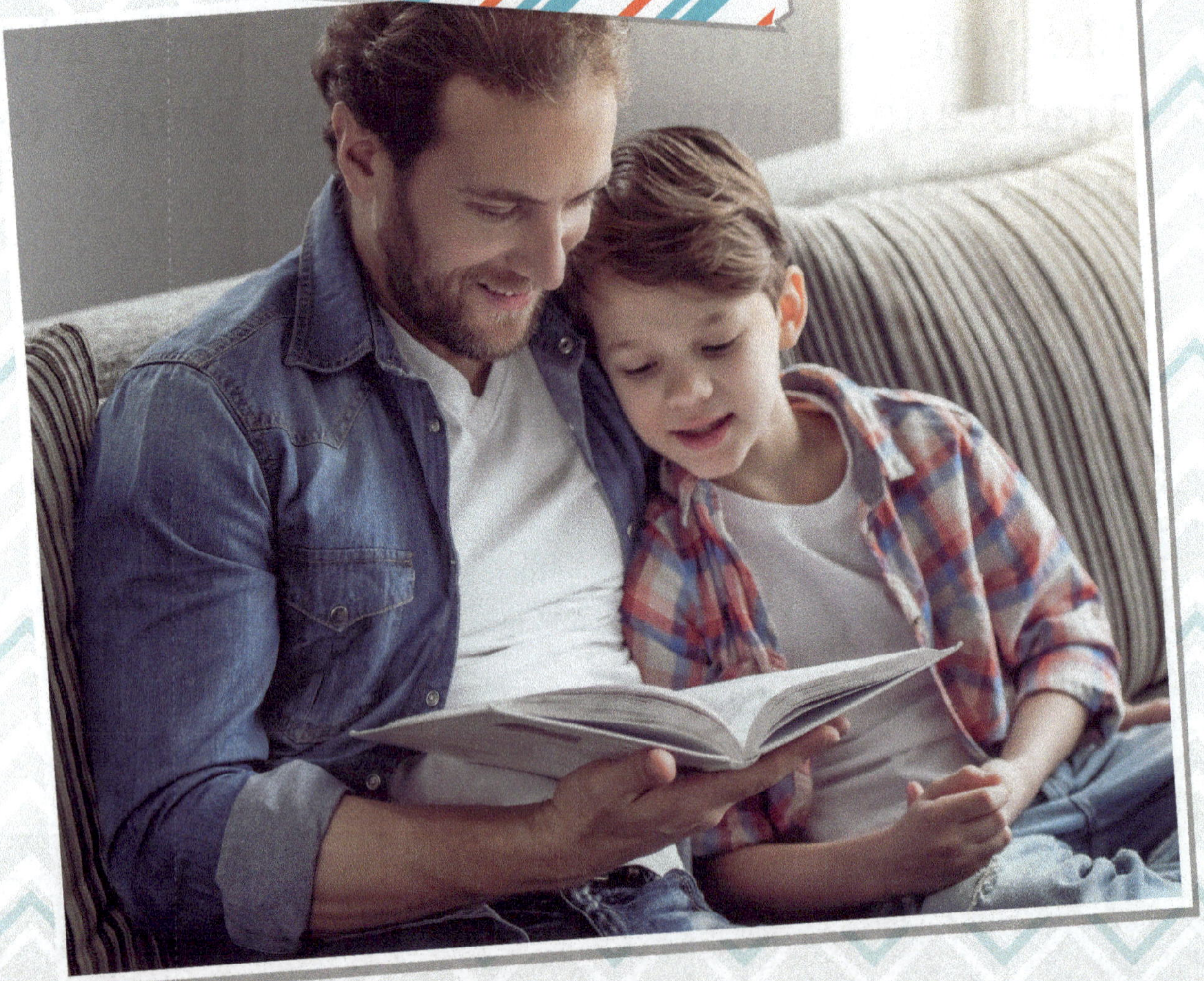

Visit

BABY PROFESSOR
EDUCATION KIDS

www.BabyProfessorBooks.com

to download Free Baby Professor eBooks and view
our catalog of new and exciting Children's Books